W9-BWU-601

DRONES

Elsie Olson

**Checkerboard
Library**

An Imprint of Abdo Publishing
abdopublishing.com

ABDOPUBLISHING.COM

Published by Abdo Publishing, a division of ABDO, PO Box 398166, Minneapolis, Minnesota 55439.
Copyright © 2018 by Abdo Consulting Group, Inc. International copyrights reserved in all countries.
No part of this book may be reproduced in any form without written permission from the publisher.
Checkerboard Library™ is a trademark and logo of Abdo Publishing.

Printed in the United States of America, North Mankato, Minnesota
062017
092017

THIS BOOK CONTAINS
RECYCLED MATERIALS

Design: Kelly Doudna, Mighty Media, Inc.
Production: Mighty Media, Inc.
Editor: Rebecca Felix
Cover Photograph: Shutterstock
Interior Photographs: Alamy, pp. 9, 12; iStockphoto, p. 5; Lauren Hughes/NASA, p. 23; Library
of Congress, pp. 7, 28 (bottom left); Mighty Media, Inc., p. 17; San Diego Air and Space Museum
Archives/Flickr, pp. 11, 28 (bottom right); Shutterstock, pp. 1, 17, 19, 20, 21, 24, 25, 27, 29 (bottom);
Wikimedia Commons, pp. 8, 13, 15, 18, 28 (top), 29 (top)

Publisher's Cataloging-in-Publication Data

Names: Olson, Elsie, author.
Title: Drones / by Elsie Olson.
Description: Minneapolis, MN : Abdo Publishing, 2018. | Series: Modern
    engineering marvels.
Identifiers: LCCN 2016962794 | ISBN 9781532110894 (lib. bdg.) |
    ISBN 9781680788747 (ebook)
Subjects: LCSH: Drone aircraft--Juvenile literature. | Technological innovations--
    Juvenile literature. | Inventions--Juvenile literature.
Classification: DDC 623.74--dc23
LC record available at http://lccn.loc.gov/2016962794

Date: 2/28/18

J 629.1326 OLS
Olson, Elsie,
Drones /

CONTENTS

It's Sunday night, and you're wrapping up your project for school tomorrow. Then, you run out of red paint. No craft stores are open in your town on Sunday nights. Is your project doomed?

Not to worry. With your dad's help, you go online and order the paint. In about 30 minutes, you hear a buzzing outside. You open the front door and watch a delivery drone place a package containing the paint on your doorstep. Your project is saved!

Drone deliveries may sound like science fiction, but some companies are already testing this service. Drones can deliver packages more quickly than human delivery drivers. They can also deliver again and again without needing a break!

Drones are also known as unmanned aerial **vehicles** (UAVs). UAVs are aircraft with no human pilot onboard. They can be operated by a controller on the ground using a remote control. Some UAVs can operate without a human controlling them.

UAVs aren't only used for delivering packages. People use them for many jobs all over the world. Drones may seem like a

Some schools have started using drones to teach students about engineering, robotics, programming, and math concepts.

super modern **technology**, but early versions of drones have been around for hundreds of years!

The first UAVs appeared nearly 250 years ago. That was when French brothers Joseph and Étienne Montgolfier launched the first hot-air balloon. In June 1783, the brothers burned wool and straw under the balloon. Hot air from the fire filled the balloon, causing it to rise and stay **airborne** for ten minutes.

As designs for hot-air balloons improved, UAVs became strong enough to carry people and instruments. In 1849, Austria controlled Venice, a former **republic** and current Italian city. The Venetians revolted against Austria. In return, Austria attacked.

The Austrian military launched nearly 200 balloons. Each balloon carried a timed bomb. The Austrians hoped the wind would carry the balloons over Venice. When the timers went off, the balloons would drop the bombs. However, the wind was too strong. Most balloons drifted past their target before dropping the bombs.

Two days later, Venice surrendered to Austrian rule. Some historians believe the UAV attack attempts were partially

The Montgolfier brothers flew a second balloon in France in September 1783. This time, the balloon had a sheep, rooster, and duck as passengers!

responsible. Although the balloons didn't strike their target, they created fear in the Venetians.

RADIO CONTROL

For many years, aircraft relied on the wind or pilot control. Then, in 1898, Serbian-American inventor Nikola Tesla created the first remote control. It was a device meant to control a small boat using radio waves. At the time, most people didn't understand how remote control **technology** could be useful. But Tesla's invention would soon pave the way for the future of UAVs.

In 1917, British engineer Archibald Low led a team that developed the first unmanned aircraft using Tesla's remote control technology. The team launched a test flight on March 21. The aircraft flew, but it crashed soon after launching. Low added a **gyroscope** to the craft. This stabilized the craft, allowing it to remain **airborne** longer.

California-based Radioplane Company developed the OQ-2A in 1935, based on Denny's design.

REGINALD DENNY

Leigh Dugmore Denny was born in Great Britain in 1891. He changed his name to Reginald to pursue a film career. He appeared in more than 100 movies. When he wasn't acting, Denny loved building model airplanes. In 1934, he started a company that made radio-controlled model airplanes. Denny thought the US military might be interested in his product. So he formed Radioplane Company. It produced larger radio-controlled airplanes. In 1938, the US military hired Denny to produce aircraft for target practice. Radioplane continued to produce radio-controlled aircraft for the military for several decades. Aviation company Northrop bought Radioplane in 1952. Denny died in 1967.

Reginald Denny and Sally Eilers in the 1931 film *Parlor, Bedroom and Bath*

In 1935, actor and **aviator** Reginald Denny developed a smaller version of a radio-controlled UAV called the Radioplane. In 1941, Denny sold 15,000 Radioplanes to the US military. They were the first UAVs to be mass produced in the United States.

LIGHTNING BUGS & PREDATORS

4

By the end of the 1950s, **technology** had improved. It had also become less expensive. As a result, the US military had even more drones developed. In 1951, Ryan **Aeronautical** Company developed the XQ-2 Firebee. This jet-**propelled** drone was used for target practice and air-to-air combat training. It could fly for nearly an hour, and higher than 50,000 feet (15,240 m).

In the 1960s, the US military created a version of the Firebee called the Lightning Bug. The Lightning Bug was used for **reconnaissance** missions during the **Vietnam War**. Because no pilot was onboard, the UAV could fly into dangerous places to gather information and return to its sender. New versions of the Firebee were created through the 1980s.

Meanwhile, in 1964, US aerospace company Lockheed Corporation released the D-21 Drone. This pilotless aircraft was designed to take photos during **surveillance** missions. The D-21's flight path was preprogrammed into the drone, including a drop-off location. After completing its mission, the drone

The first Firebee models could travel at speeds of more than 500 mph (805 kmh)!

would release a package containing film of the images it took. The drone would then self-destruct. And the US military would recover the package at the drop-off location.

By the 1980s, **technology** and computers had improved greatly. The US military began working to improve its drones. It built drones that could fly faster, travel farther, and stay **airborne** longer than previous UAVs.

In 1988, a drone called the Condor made by US **aviation** company Boeing broke a record. It became the first aircraft to remain airborne for nearly two and a half days without refueling, and to reach a height of more than 65,000 feet (19,800 m).

By the mid-1990s, UAVs had become an important part of US military operations. In 1994, the Predator UAV went on its first test flight. This would become one of the most important UAVs in US history.

By 2001, Predators were armed with **missiles**. They were also equipped with **reconnaissance** equipment. This gave them the ability to

The United States isn't the only country to use Predator drones. Canada, France, Germany, Italy, Spain, Bosnia, and more also use Predator models.

accurately locate and hit targets. Predators played an important role during conflicts in the Middle East in the early 2000s. They also paved the way for future US-made armed UAVs, including the Reaper and the Gray Eagle.

5 MILITARY DRONES

Since drones were developed, they have played an important role in military operations. The military uses UAVs for unsafe operations that might risk soldiers' lives. Some drones are made to be carried in a soldier's backpack. Others are the size of a plane and cost millions of dollars. They can fly for up to 17 hours.

Military drones serve many purposes. Some are used for **surveillance**, intelligence gathering, and mapping **terrain**. Other drones carry bombs or **missiles**. Pilots on the ground hundreds of miles away fly these drones into enemy territory. The pilots drop bombs and missiles on targets without risking their lives.

Missile-carrying drones help protect US soldiers. The drone pilots are far away from the areas the drones enter. The pilots rely on images provided by the drone. It can be hard to identify enemies from other people in these images. As a result, drones don't always attack their planned targets. Thousands of **civilians** have been accidentally killed by drone attacks.

A US soldier launches a Raven in Iraq in 2007. This small observation drone is the most widely used UAV in the world.

The drones used throughout history came in many shapes and sizes. Modern drones do as well, and they serve many purposes. But all drones have a few things in common.

Drones come in two main styles. These are fixed wing and **rotary**. Fixed wing drones resemble airplanes. They have a set of wings and a **propeller** that faces forward. Fixed wing drones can travel longer and farther than most rotary drones. They are also faster. However, they often require a runway to take off.

Rotary drones are usually smaller than fixed wing drones. They are designed more like helicopters. Most rotary drones have four propellers. Some have up to eight. The propellers sit on top of the drone.

Multiple propellers give the drone more lift. This allows the drone to carry heavier equipment than a drone with a single propeller. More propellers also give the drone more stability. In addition, unlike fixed wing drones, rotary drones are able to hover in the air.

THE PREDATOR UAV

The Predator UAV is a fixed wing drone mainly used by the US Air Force.

AVIONICS
Radar, GPS, and computers are used to control the Predator.

WINGSPAN
The Predator has a wingspan of 48.7 feet (14.8 m).

ENGINE
The engine in a Predator is the same type used in snowmobiles.

PROPELLER
The **propeller** spins and creates lift and forward motion.

CAMERA SENSOR ARRAY
The camera sensor array is a group of sensors that collect images.

FUSELAGE
The fuselage is the body of an aircraft. The Predator has a narrow fuselage.

RUDDER
The rudder steers the Predator.

V-SHAPED TAIL
The V shape gives the Predator better stability.

Many military drones are controlled by pilots thousands of miles away. These pilots receive extensive classroom and hands-on training.

All drones have a power source. Many **rotary** drones use batteries. Most battery-powered drones can fly for a maximum of 25 minutes. A longer fly time requires a bigger battery, which weighs the drone down. To get a longer flight time, most fixed wing drones use fuel-powered engines. These drones are usually larger and can fly for hours without refueling.

TALKING TO DRONES

All drones also have a human controller who helps the drone take off and land. The controller communicates with the drone using radio waves or Wi-Fi. This can include smartphones or a small remote control. Controllers of larger, military drones use powerful computers. Instructions can also be preprogrammed into the drone.

However, GPS and navigation systems allow drones to perform many functions without human guidance. **Accelerometers** measure tilt and acceleration. And **gyroscopes** detect the drone's angular velocity and orientation. These sensors keep the drone **airborne**. They also allow the drone to adjust for changes in the weather, such as wind gusts.

The main difference between a remote control helicopter and a rotary drone is that a drone can fly, hover, or navigate independently.

Drones can fly, hover, and carry a camera. Because of this, the film industry has adopted drone **technology** for many aerial shots. Before drones, many of these shots had to be taken by a photographer inside a helicopter. Fuel and crew costs to fly a helicopter can reach $25,000 per day. A drone and its crew costs as little as $5,000 per day.

Because of their smaller size, drones can also get closer to the action than helicopters. Drones can fly behind waterfalls, alongside a skier racing down a hill, and more. Movies including *Skyfall, Transformers 4: Age of Extinction, Fast and Furious 6,* and the Harry Potter films all used drones to film certain scenes. Drones are also often used to film commercials with a lot of action. Drones are also used to film sporting

TECH TIDBIT

In 2016, pop star Rihanna released a music video featuring drone footage for her song "Sledgehammer."

Rotary drones' ability to hover in the air makes them perfect for photography and filming.

events. They are small and quick enough to get close to the action without interfering with the game. The music industry has also started using drones to film music videos.

8 DRONES AT WORK

Drones have other amazing jobs outside of the film industry. Farmers have used dogs to herd sheep for hundreds of years. But some farmers are now using drones instead. The farmer operates the drone using a remote control. A camera feed shows him or her what the drone is seeing. The drones can travel over hilly **terrain** to find sheep more quickly than dogs.

Drones are also useful for activities that are too dangerous for human pilots. In 2016, **NASA** used a Global Hawk drone to study Hurricane Matthew. The drone dropped instruments directly into the hurricane. The instruments sent wind speed, temperature, and other information to NASA. Such a mission would have been very dangerous for a human pilot to attempt.

Other dangerous jobs drones have taken on include photographing erupting volcanoes and finding alligator nests. Drones can enter the nest to measure and record other information about alligators without putting humans in danger. Drones have also been used to monitor for shark activity on

NASA has used Global Hawk drones to monitor hurricanes and other extreme weather since 2010. The drones can travel for up to 30 hours without refueling.

beaches. This allows officials to close a swimming beach if a shark is nearby.

As drones have grown more common, many models have become less expensive. This has allowed them to find a market with regular consumers. In fact, in 2016, more than 2.5 million drones were sold to US hobbyists. Hobby drones come in a wide range of prices and sizes. Some hobby drones cost as little as $35. Others cost more than $1,000.

Some hobby drones come with expensive cameras. Others come with camera mounts, so users can add their own cameras. Certain hobby drones are designed especially for racing. Others are made just as fun toys. They can be flown like remote-controlled model airplanes and helicopters.

TECH TIDBIT

In 2015, a Washington, DC, man accidentally landed a drone on the White House lawn. Fortunately, no one was hurt.

DRONE RESTRICTIONS

As hobby drones become more popular, they also come with risks. If they enter

the airspace of planes and helicopters, drones can affect the navigation systems of these aircraft or cause crashes. Drones can also damage power lines, buildings, and even hurt people if the operator isn't careful.

Globally, people spent about $200 million on drones in 2016! Sales are expected to rise from 2.5 million drones in 2016 to 7 million in 2020.

Because of these concerns, the government has created rules about where drones can be flown. Operators must register any drones weighing more than 0.55 pounds (0.25 kg) with the Federal **Aviation** Administration before using them. Drone owners are not allowed to fly drones at night, over crowded areas, or too close to an airport without the airport's permission.

Some drone makers build **restrictions** into their drones. If the drone gets too close to an airport or other restricted area, the drone will **automatically** land.

Experts expect drones to become more and more popular as drone **technology** keeps improving. In 2013, online retail company Amazon.com announced that it was exploring drone delivery. Other retail companies, including Wal-Mart and Google, are exploring similar drone delivery options. The company Zipline launched in 2014. It uses drones to deliver needed medical supplies to remote areas.

Some law enforcement groups have started using drones in search and rescue efforts. Future police drones could even be equipped with stun guns. The drones would be able to respond to threats more quickly, and may be able to handle dangerous situations without putting officers' lives in danger. However, some are concerned that police drones would be more **intrusive** than human officers, and would violate citizens' privacy.

People have also proposed using drones to wait tables, monitor **endangered** animals, help with construction projects, map areas damaged by natural disasters, and more. Social media

Amazon's drone delivery system is called Prime Air. It aims to deliver packages weighing up to five pounds (2 kg) in 30 minutes or less.

company Facebook has even discussed using drones to broadcast Internet connections in remote areas. Drones will continue to play an important role in US military operations. What else might drones of the future do? Almost anything you can imagine!

TECH TIMELINE

1849

The Austrian military launches nearly 200 balloons carrying timed bombs to attack the republic of Venice.

1935

Reginald Denny develops a radio-controlled UAV called the Radioplane.

1783

Brothers Joseph and Étienne Montgolfier launch the first hot-air balloon.

1898

Nikola Tesla creates the first remote control.

1951

Ryan Aeronautical Company creates the XQ-2 Firebee.

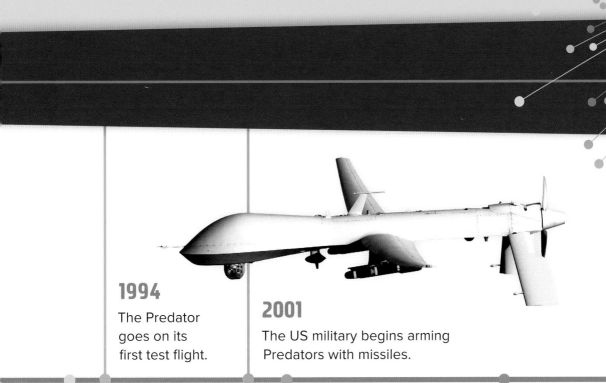

1994
The Predator goes on its first test flight.

2001
The US military begins arming Predators with missiles.

1964
Lockheed Corporation releases the D-21 Drone.

2013
Amazon announces that it is experimenting with using drones to deliver packages.

2016
NASA uses a Global Hawk drone to study Hurricane Matthew.

GLOSSARY

accelerometer–an instrument for measuring acceleration or vibration.

aeronautical–related to the science dealing with the design, manufacture, and operation of aircraft.

airborne–supported or transported by air.

automatic–moving or acting by itself.

aviation–the operation and navigation of aircraft. A person who operates aircraft is called an aviator.

civilian–a person who is not an active member of the military.

endangered–in danger of becoming extinct.

gyroscope–a wheel or disk mounted to spin quickly about an axis that is free to turn in various directions.

intrusive–entering without being asked or wanted.

missile–a weapon that is thrown or projected to hit a target.

NASA–National Aeronautics and Space Administration. NASA is a US government agency that manages the nation's space program and conducts flight research.

propel–to drive forward or onward by some force. A device with spinning blades that propel a vehicle is a propeller.

reconnaissance–an inspection used by the military to gain information about enemy territory.

republic–a form of government in which citizens elect leaders to manage the government.

restrict–to keep within certain limits. Something that does this is a restriction.

rotary–having a part that turns on an axis like a wheel.

surveillance–close watch kept over someone or something.

technology–a capability given by the practical application of knowledge.

terrain–the natural features of an area of land, such as mountains and rivers.

vehicle–something used to carry or transport. Cars, trucks, airplanes, and boats are vehicles.

Vietnam War–from 1957 to 1975. A long, failed attempt by the United States to stop North Vietnam from taking over South Vietnam.

WEBSITES

To learn more about Modern Engineering Marvels, visit **abdobooklinks.com**. These links are routinely monitored and updated to provide the most current information available.

INDEX